OUT
OF THE
BAG

OUT OF

THE
PAPER
BAG
PLAYERS
BOOK
OF PLAYS

THE BAG

ILLUSTRATED BY SEYMOUR CHWAST

BY JUDITH MARTIN

Hyperion Books
for Children
New York

*For Donald Ashwander,
composer and musician for the
Paper Bag Players
for 28 years. His joyful music
and presence will be
remembered by thousands
of children and their parents.*

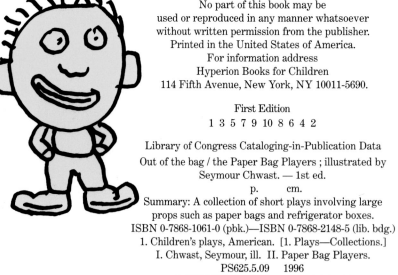

First Edition
1 3 5 7 9 10 8 6 4 2

Library of Congress Cataloging-in-Publication Data
Out of the bag / the Paper Bag Players ; illustrated by
Seymour Chwast. — 1st ed.
p.   cm.
Summary: A collection of short plays involving large
props such as paper bags and refrigerator boxes.
ISBN 0-7868-1061-0 (pbk.)—ISBN 0-7868-2148-5 (lib. bdg.)
1. Children's plays, American. [1. Plays—Collections.]
I. Chwast, Seymour, ill. II. Paper Bag Players.
PS625.5.09   1996
812'.540809282—dc20   94-46006

CONTENTS

Introduction

by Judith Martin

The Paper Bag Players was formed quite spontaneously in 1958. A few friends and I—a dancer, an actress, a painter, and an illustrator—met in a small studio solely for the fun of making up theater pieces. Our stories were all original, some made up as we went along. Our costumes were made from cardboard boxes gathered from neighborhood stores or found in the street. Props were usually household objects that happened to be around. We were all drawn to humor and fantasy and thought children would be our ideal audience. Very quickly we put together a whole program and soon after were invited to give daytime shows at an Off-Broadway theater that in the evening was a home for contemporary plays.

We were surprised and pleased to find ourselves getting a great deal of attention in the press, hailed as innovators in the field of children's theater. At that time children's theater was inhabited mainly by velvet-robed kings and queens, fairy godmothers, ugly goblins, beautiful princesses, and wicked stepmothers. In our plays, all the actors looked like ordinary people. There was only one queen and she was funny and dressed in paper. The hero of our main story was a meatball, and throughout the show, the audience got to tell people on the stage what to do.

Since then, for some thirty years, we have been creating plays, stage paintings, songs, and dances, and performing them for children throughout the United States, Canada, and in countries in Europe, Asia, and the Far East. Now we are very excited to have some of our favorite plays illustrated by Seymour Chwast and printed in a book for children themselves to perform.

When putting on a play, the first task is to settle on a subject that intrigues the actors. Everyday home life is a familiar setting for humorous conflict, so this book includes several plays about common but dramatic events like cleaning a bedroom or taking a bath. For a more poetic view of life, there are also plays here about nature and the earth's environment. If the young actors are excited about the theme of the play, it's off to a good start.

Supplying the actors with their costumes early in rehearsals gives an immediate feeling of excitement and theatricality. It also allows the child to make the costumes an intrinsic part of his performance from the start. We have chosen plays that have few words, lots of action, and easy-to-make costumes. Each play is short, but a few of them put together would make a full theater piece with parts for actors of all sizes and shapes.

Putting on a play can be like playing a great game —a game that anybody can join. Children can choose to sing or act or dance or paint scenery or make costumes or even sell tickets. Putting on a show with friends is fun for everyone because in a good play everyone is important.

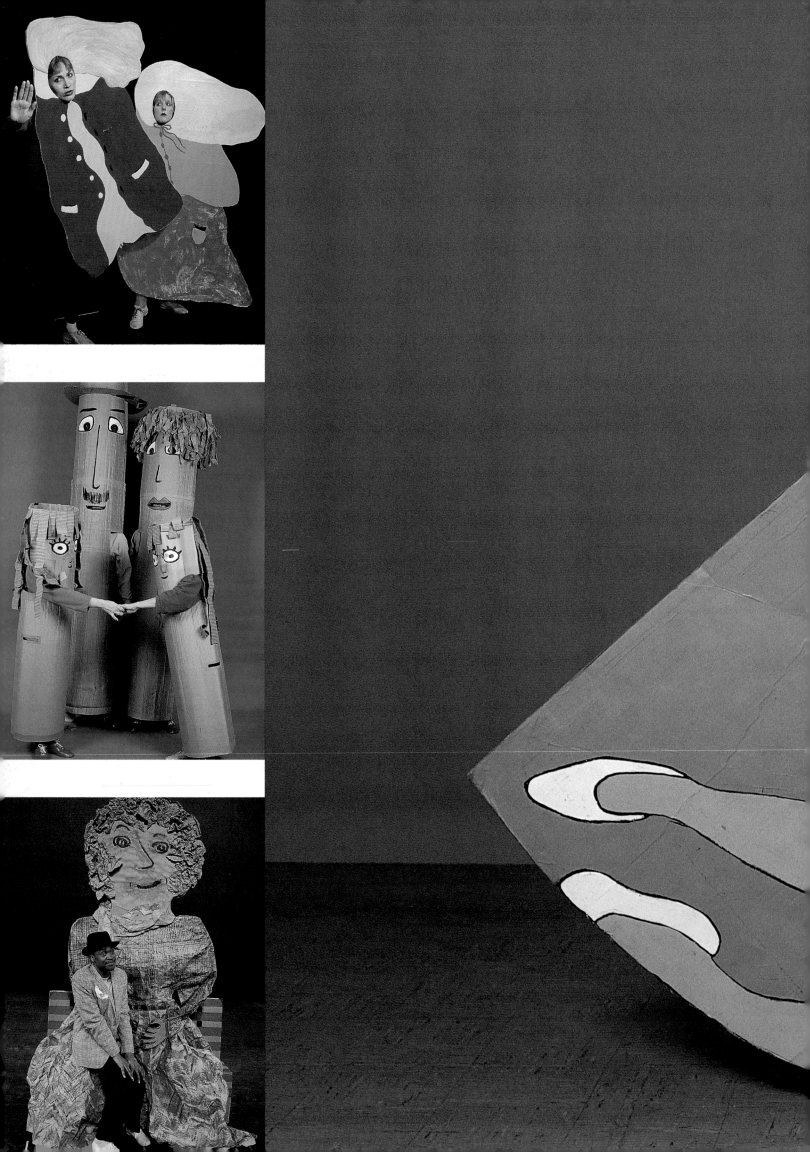

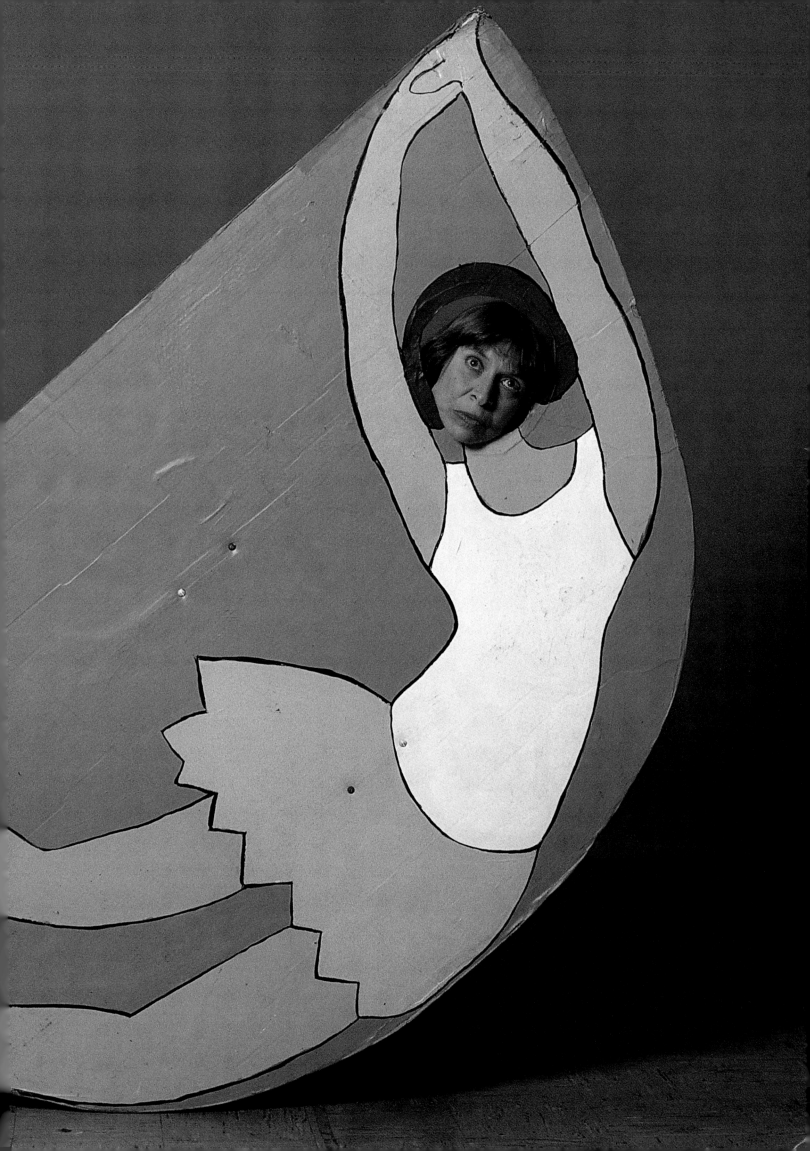

Getting Started

Used cardboard boxes for making costumes are readily available from local stores. For ordinary sizes, grocery and drugstores are the best sources. For large pieces of cardboard, furniture and appliance stores are the places to look. Almost always there is someone in charge who will save large boxes for you or tell you the best day to come for them. Get someone to help you carry them home. Be sure to get more cardboard than you think you need—after all, it's free! If you make a mistake, you can just throw it out. With lots of cardboard you will be surprised how easy it will be to get started.

Costumes and Props

In plays, an actor may portray an animal, a flower, a tree, something grand like the sun or the moon, or something silly like a bathtub.

The Paper Bag Players have always used paper and cardboard for their costumes and props. They are the same materials you might find at home. Many things your parents buy come in boxes that they do not need.

Each play requires different costumes and props. So follow the directions carefully.

It is best to sketch an outline on your paper or cardboard first. Cut out your design with a pair of scissors and color it with poster (tempera) paints, which you can get at an art supply store. You can mix the colors easily and any mess can be cleaned up with water. Whatever you make is ready to use as soon as the paint is dry.

MIXING COLORS

You can make all the colors you need with black, white, red, yellow and blue paints. Be sure to wash your brush in water before changing colors.

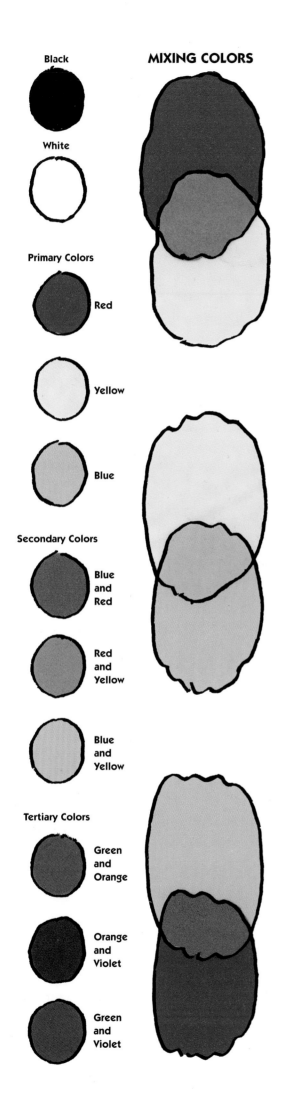

Black

White

Primary Colors

Red

Yellow

Blue

Secondary Colors

Blue and Red

Red and Yellow

Blue and Yellow

Tertiary Colors

Green and Orange

Orange and Violet

Green and Violet

MIXING DISHES

WATER

NEWSPAPER

4

5

CHARACTERS
FATHER
MOTHER
CHILD #1
CHILD #2

LOST IN A MALL

COSTUMES
A mask for each member of the cast.

A bare stage with an exit on each side.
(FATHER enters in search of his wife.)

FATHER Darling! Dearest!
(to audience) Have you seen my wife?
(Audience answers.) I can't find her anywhere.

FATHER exits, MOTHER enters.

MOTHER Darling! Darling!
(to audience) Have you seen my husband?
(Audience answers.) Which way did he go?
(Audience answers. MOTHER starts in one direction
but gets confused.) This way?

(Audience answers. MOTHER turns around and
starts off in the wrong direction. Just as MOTHER is
about to exit, FATHER appears across stage.)

FATHER Darling!

MOTHER Dearest.

They meet center stage and hug.

MOTHER Where are the children?

FATHER I thought they were with you.

MOTHER I thought they were with you!

FATHER (to audience) Have you seen our
children? (Audience answers.)

FATHER and MOTHER (calling offstage)
Children! Children!

FATHER I'll look this way.

MOTHER I'll look that way.

They start off in different directions, but
get confused and end up exiting into
the same wing.

The CHILDREN enter.

CHILDREN (to audience) Have you seen our
parents? (Audience answers.) Which way did
they go? (Audience answers. CHILDREN exit.
MOTHER enters.)

MOTHER Children! Children!
(to audience) Have you seen my babies?
(Audience answers.) Which way did they go?
(Audience answers.) This way? This way?
Ohhh!

MOTHER exits. CHILDREN enter.

CHILD #1 Mama!

CHILD #2 Papa!

CHILD #1 Mama!

CHILD #2 Papa!

CHILD #1 Mama!

CHILD #2 Papa!

MOTHER and FATHER enter.

MOTHER and FATHER Children!

CHILD #1 Mama!

CHILD #1 Papa!
They all meet center stage and hug.

MOTHER Where were you?

CHILD #1 I was here. Where were you?

FATHER I was here. Where were you?

Child #2 I was here. Where were you?

MOTHER Never mind. We're all together now.
They hold hands and exit.

The Big Mess

COSTUMES

MOTHER. A housedress.

TED. A sweatshirt.

THE MESS. A huge, irregular paper bag, large enough for an actor to get into, lift his arms and whirl around in, and not be seen. There must be eyeholes for the actor to see out. The bag should be painted with all sorts of colors, shapes, and crisscross lines, to suggest a heap of clothes, toys, schoolbooks, sporting equipment, and junk.

PROPS

CLOSET. A large cardboard wardrobe closet, made of two refrigerator boxes. It must accommodate an actor with outstretched hands. The closet must have double doors and no bottom.

BROOM.

17

The closet glides onto an empty stage. It is being pushed by an actor inside. It stops center stage.

MOTHER (**Enters. She looks about room and is elated by what she sees.**) I can't believe it. It's happened! It has actually happened. My son has cleaned his room. Ah . . . I'm just going to take a little peek inside the closet. (**Opens closet door. THE MESS falls out of closet and sprawls on the floor. MOTHER is horrified.**) What a mess! I just don't understand. I am a very clean, very neat person. My husband is a very neat person, and I believe that children take after their parents. So I cannot explain why my son, my own son, has the messiest, the sloppiest, the most disgusting-looking room in our neighborhood. Ted, Ted, where are you?

TED (**Enters.**) Ma, what's up?

MOTHER Ted, look at this mess. It's horrible, it's hideous, it's . . . it's depressing.

TED Ma, don't get so excited. It's not so bad.

MOTHER Not so bad?

TED I think it's okay.

MOTHER Well, I think it's a mess.

TED But Ma, if it doesn't bother me, why should it bother you?

MOTHER It bothers me. It bothers me because it doesn't make any sense. How can you find anything?

TED I know where everything is. Just ask me.

MOTHER Ted, I'm not getting into a discussion with you. This is an order—you are going to stay in your room until this place is neat and tidy, and I don't care if you stay here six months. I never want to see that mess again. (**She gets the broom from the wing.**) Here is a broom. Now clean your room, and that is final. (**Exits.**)

TED Gee, I don't know what she's so excited about. But if that's what she wants, I'll get rid of this mess in a minute.

With three short brushstrokes he sweeps THE MESS across the floor. Pleased with himself, he walks back to where he started.

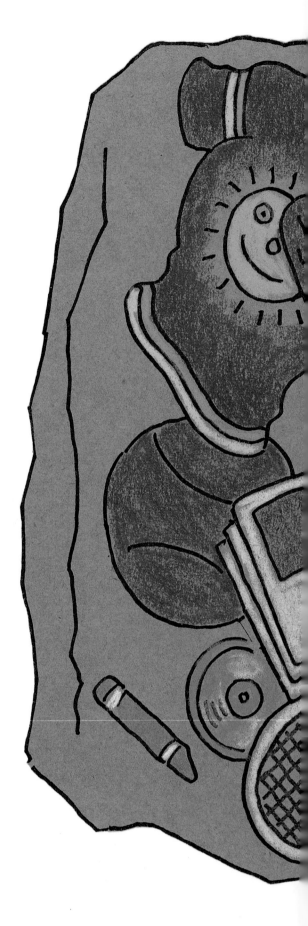

TED There! (THE MESS creeps back to TED and wraps itself around TED's legs.) What kind of a game is this? (TED climbs over THE MESS and takes firm hold of the broom.) We may have a fight on our hands.

He sweeps again with an angry motion. Each sweep of the broom causes THE MESS to move and swirl around, finally curling up in a tight ball.

TED See, Mess, I'm the boss around here!

THE MESS uncurls and reaches its total height, then chases TED around the stage, pauses, opens to its full width, envelopes TED, and presses him to the ground. TED, now on the floor, is covered by THE MESS. He pushes it away enough to raise his head and call.

TED Ma! Ma! (THE MESS again covers him.)

MOTHER (Enters. Does not see TED.) This is worse than when I left. Ted, Ted, where are you?

TED (just his head appearing from under THE MESS) Ma, this is too much for me.

MOTHER (helping him up) Ted, dear, this is what happens when you don't pick up a little every day.

TED Ma! I can't handle this.

MOTHER This is the last time I'm going to help you. (Takes broom from TED.) Ted, you are old enough and big enough to clean your own room. (to audience) He is so spoiled.

TED (to THE MESS) Okay, Mess, you've met your match.

MOTHER Now Ted, watch. A little sweep to the left, a little sweep to the right. Sweep, sweep, sweep. (THE MESS moves a little with each sweep.) That does it!

THE MESS swirls and towers over MOTHER. MOTHER screams.

TED See, I told you it wasn't easy.

MOTHER Well, it's because of all this junk around here!

THE MESS seems to be retreating.

TED Ma, it's getting away.

THE MESS suddenly turns and threatens MOTHER.

MOTHER Get away from me. (Swings broom.)

TED Ma, Ma! Take it easy.

MOTHER (to THE MESS) Don't you come near me. Don't you come near me.

TED Be careful, Ma. Take it easy.
(THE MESS circles MOTHER, then backs off. MOTHER faints and falls to the floor. TED, like a referee, begins to count.) One, two, three . . . (MOTHER rises.) Ma, Ma are you all right?

MOTHER I'm perfectly all right. I want that Mess out of here.

TED Oh, Mess is in big trouble now.

MOTHER (Attacks THE MESS.) Just take this— sweep! And another sweep! And one more sweep!

THE MESS runs behind the closet.

TED Ma, it's getting away.

TED and MOTHER chase THE MESS, which has disappeared behind the closet.

MOTHER Get it, get it!

TED and MOTHER come from behind the closet. They have not found THE MESS.

TED Where did it go? I don't see it.

Suddenly THE MESS appears again from behind the closet.

MOTHER That way.

They chase THE MESS again around the closet. They grab THE MESS's costume. The actor slips into the closet.

TED Pull, pull on it, Ma.

MOTHER I don't want to touch it.

MOTHER and TED shake out THE MESS. It's a paper shell with no actor in it.

MOTHER Let's get rid of it. (They shove it into the closet and raise their hands in a victory sign.)

BOTH We did it! We did it!
(Arms around each other, they exit.)

The closet with THE MESS inside exits in the opposite direction.

CHARACTERS
GIRL
ICE
SUN
CLOUD
SEED (FLOWER)
NIGHT

SUN & ICE

COSTUMES

GIRL. A hat with earmuffs, sunglasses, and a sweater.

Also, a flower for her to hold.

ICE. A large square made of waxed paper strips, taped together so it can be worn like a poncho.

CLOUD. A cardboard cutout shaped like a cloud, painted white and gray. It has hand holes and is carried by an actor.

The CLOUD actor wears a shower cap and carries a stick with tinsel strips taped to it and hanging from it. The tinsel hanging from the stick looks like rain.

NIGHT. A very large rectangle, made of paper and painted blue with silver stars, to be worn like a cape. Attached to each end, at the top of the paper, are two sticks. When NIGHT opens his cape, the blue paper billows.

SUN. A large cardboard circle, carried by an actor. It is painted yellow. An extra half-circle is glued onto it; the side flap cannot be noticed. When the SUN sets, the extra flap turns down. The inside of the flap is painted red, as is the part of the SUN concealed by the flap, so that the SUN appears to be turning red.

— FLAP

— FLAP

SEED. A collar, worn over the actor's head. It is made of heavy brown paper, cut in the shape of a flower, and painted a brilliant color. The reverse side is painted tan so when the petals are folded, the costume looks like a seed.

Enter GIRL wearing the hat, sunglasses, and sweater and holding the flower.

GIRL Winter, spring, summer, fall.
Winter, spring, summer, fall.
Winter, spring, summer, fall.

As she speaks she points in turn to her hat, her flower, her sunglasses, and her sweater. ICE enters. He goes directly to GIRL and towers above her.

ICE Not this year.

GIRL This year winter refused to leave.

ICE Why should I?

GIRL, intimidated, exits.

ICE The whole world is cold and white and beautiful. Lakes are frozen. Mountains are covered with snow. Icicles hang from the trees. I am the most powerful force on Earth.

SUN enters and moves across the stage in a circular pattern. SUN's movements are happy and cheerful. SUN ends up very close to ICE.

SUN With one exception.

ICE It's the sun! He's going to ruin everything.

SUN You've made everything cold, hard, and still—but I'm going to warm things up, make them move and grow.

ICE Don't make me laugh. He's going to make things ugly.

SUN Ugly? Why, I make flowers grow. And heat waves. I also make it hot.

As they argue, ICE tries to cover SUN, and SUN tries to cover ICE.

ICE I make snow and blizzards.

SUN I make it hot.

ICE I make it cold.

SUN Hot.

ICE Cold.

SUN Hot.

(sound of thunder from offstage)

SUN Thunder!

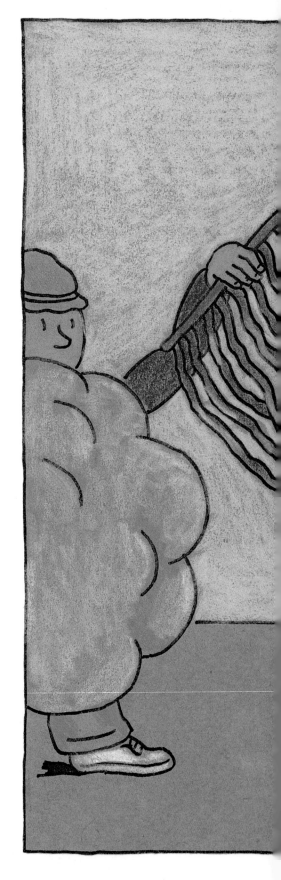

CLOUD enters. The stick with the hanging strips of tinsel is hidden behind the cardboard cutout.

CLOUD What's going on here? Cold, hot, hot, cold, hot, hot, hot, cold, cold, cold. I can't even make a decent rainstorm anymore.

SUN It's springtime and he won't leave.

ICE Why should I? I have a right to be here.

SUN What are you talking about? It's time for the earth to warm up.

CLOUD Listen to me, Ice. You've been here all winter—and it's been a long winter. Now don't you think it's time for you to get going?

ICE No! No! I don't think it's time for me to go.

SEED enters, wearing the collar with the flower petals folded.

SEED Where, where, where can I find a spot to plant myself?

SUN What is it?

CLOUD It's a seed.

SUN A seed!

CLOUD A little seed.

SEED I'm looking for a place to get started, but the ground is so cold and hard! Sun, can't you warm things up—just a bit?

SUN (moving close to CLOUD) Excuse me, Cloud, this little seed needs me.

SEED (to SUN) What's Ice doing here? He shouldn't be here.

SUN You heard her, Ice, it's time for you to go.

Now SUN feels very powerful and chases ICE around the stage.

SUN Melt! Melt!

ICE I'm turning to slush.

SUN Melt!

ICE I'm going, but I'll be back.

ICE exits.

SUN (to SEED) Now you can start growing.

SEED Just in time. My roots are itching and my leaves are ready to pop. I've got to grow, I just can't stop. I need some sun.

SUN The sun is here. **(Makes a circular movement around SEED, suggesting sun rays.)** How's that?

SEED I feel dry.

CLOUD You need rain. **(Produces the stick and waves it up and down in front of SEED.)** How does that feel?

SEED I'm soggy.

SUN (circling SEED) Sun.

CLOUD (repeating motions with tinsel) Rain.

SUN (sun movements) Sun.

CLOUD (rain movements) Rain.

SUN (sun movements) Sun.

CLOUD (rain movements) Rain.

SUN How's that feel?

SEED That feels just right.

SUN I think it's time. Come on, little Seed, you can do it. **(The SEED costume unfolds and, a petal at a time, becomes a brilliantly colored FLOWER.)** Come on, you're almost there. Come on. **(FLOWER is fully opened.)** Well done, little Flower!

CLOUD Oh little Flower, you look pretty good. I'm done in, I'm all wiped out. **(Exits with a heavy, weary walk.)**

SUN The seed has become a flower, and it's a beautiful day.

Enter NIGHT.

NIGHT No day is complete without me.

SUN Night, I forgot about you.

NIGHT It's the end of the day, why do you delay?

SUN I do not delay, but I must leave in a certain way.

The SUN crosses the stage to exit. The yellow cardboard circle that SUN carries is raised very high. The top half unfolds, and the circle becomes red. It slowly lowers.

SUN I'll be back the first thing in the morning.

NIGHT (grudgingly) Not bad, not bad at all. And in the meantime it will be night, and nothing is as beautiful as a star-filled sky. **(Opens his cape, raises it high above his head, and sweeps around the stage. At one point the FLOWER is behind NIGHT and exits unseen by the audience. NIGHT, alone on the stage, circles once more and exits.)**

Sandwich

COSTUMES

WAITER. A white apron.

MISS LITTLE. A hat and pocket-book.

MRS. BIGG. A hat and pocketbook.

PROPS

TABLE. A cardboard box on which are painted four legs and a tablecloth.

SANDWICH. Cardboard boxes glued together and painted to look like a sandwich. It should be a little bigger than the tabletop.

CHARACTERS

WAITER
MISS LITTLE
MRS. BIGG

SETTING

A BARE STAGE. WAITER enters carrying table. With elegant gestures he sets it down and smoothes tablecloth. Exits.

MISS LITTLE enters. There is no chair at the table, but she sits as if there were one. She acts as if she has a plate of food and with delicate and rhythmic gestures cuts it, brings it to her mouth, and chews it.

MRS. BIGG enters and also sits at the table as if there were a chair.

WAITER enters, stands at table, acts as if he has a pad and pencil, and takes MRS. BIGG's order.

MRS. BIGG Waiter, I'd like to order, please. Would you bring me a ham sandwich on thin-sliced whole wheat toast with a dab of mayonnaise . . . and a slice of chicken would be good . . . a few pieces of roast beef and a few pieces of salami . . . don't forget the ketchup . . . some Swiss cheese, some cream cheese . . . lettuce, tomato, and cucumber . . . mustard and relish, a little peanut butter and jelly to top that off, with a few sardines. That'll be all.

WAITER exits to fill order. MISS LITTLE resumes eating because she stopped and listened with amazement to MRS. BIGG's order. WAITER returns carrying the sandwich. He sets it on the table. It is bigger than the tabletop.

MRS. BIGG (surprised and somewhat distressed) Waiter, is that my sandwich?

WAITER That's it. **(He exits.)**

MISS LITTLE It's perfectly beautiful. Can I have a piece?

MRS. BIGG Why no, that's my sandwich.

MISS LITTLE (pleading) Just a bite.

MRS. BIGG Take your hands off my sandwich!

MISS LITTLE and MRS. BIGG grab opposite sides of the sandwich and pull back and forth in a tug-of-war.

MRS. BIGG It's my sandwich!

MISS LITTLE Don't be greedy.

They continue their argument and tug-of-war until, abruptly, MISS LITTLE falls backward and lands on the floor, with the sandwich on top of her.

MRS. BIGG HELP! WAITER!

WAITER What happened?

MRS. BIGG That woman is under my sandwich. I'm never coming to this place again. The service is terrible!

WAITER Now wait just a minute, lady. You ordered that sandwich, and that sandwich is yours.

MRS. BIGG I don't want that sandwich. I don't want it.

WAITER lifts sandwich off MISS LITTLE, who is still on the floor under sandwich, and thrusts it upon MRS. BIGG.

WAITER Now get that sandwich out of here.

MISS LITTLE (Gets up from floor. Sympathetically rushes to MRS. BIGG and helps her hold sandwich.) Don't worry, dear.

MRS. BIGG How will I get this home?

MISS LITTLE I'll help you.

MRS. BIGG But I live in Queens.

Now the sandwich is on MISS LITTLE's back, and MRS. BIGG is holding up one end. They are on their way to MRS. BIGG's home.

MISS LITTLE Oh, that's all right. I have friends in Queens.

Exit both women with sandwich.

PROPS

BINOCULARS
A BUTTERFLY NET
A BIG BOOK
that identifies
birds, flowers,
and animals.

COSTUMES

MAN. Hunter's cap.

Hands Off! Don't Touch!

SETTING

The play takes place in an imaginary forest.
It is possible to use a blank stage or a
background painted with trees and flowers.

CHARACTERS

BIRD (never seen, but
heard from offstage)
MAN (a bird-watcher,
collector of flowers
and butterflies)
FLOWER
BUTTERFLY
LION

NOTE: Though the play
is written for one butterfly
and one flower, the cast
could easily be expanded
for several butterflies and
several flowers.

Enter MAN. He wears binoculars and is carrying the butterfly net and book. He walks about, trying not to make any noise. He stops and looks through his binoculars whenever he hears a bird whistle. The bird is never seen; all its sounds come from offstage.

BIRD Brrrp, brrp.

MAN That's the sound of a yellow-bellied nutcracker!

BIRD Wrooop, wrooop.

MAN And that's the red-headed hoodwinker!

Enter FLOWER. She takes small dainty steps, wandering about the stage. The MAN follows her every movement. The FLOWER suddenly realizes the presence of MAN and stops abruptly.

MAN What do I see blooming right in front of me? A double-decker cornucopia with stamen and pistils! I must have it for my collection!

FLOWER Pick me if you must, but before you do, may I please have a few last words?

MAN Of course.

FLOWER (singing) Hands off! Don't touch! I don't ask much—Hands off! Don't touch! You'll get in dutch!

MAN (amazed) What did you say?

FLOWER (singing again) Hands off! Don't touch! I don't ask much—Hands off! Don't touch! You'll get in dutch!

MAN (Still can't believe his ears. To audience) What did that flower say?

AUDIENCE (shouting) Hands off! Don't touch! I don't ask much—Hands off! Don't touch! You'll get in dutch!

While the audience is shouting at MAN, FLOWER tiptoes away. When MAN looks around, FLOWER is gone.

MAN That flower talks too much anyway!

Enter BUTTERFLY, gently moving its wings as it circles stage. It finally settles, and MAN leaps to it and raises his butterfly net.

MAN By Jove! A super-cholesterol-ruby-winged monarch! An entomologist's dream come true. I must have it for my collection.

BUTTERFLY Add me to your collection if you must, but before you do, may I please have a few last words?

FLOWER

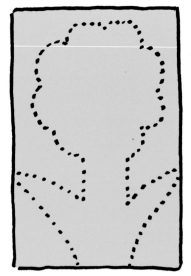

Cut on dotted line.

MAN Of course.

BUTTERFLY (singing) Hands off! Don't touch!
I don't ask much—Hands off! Don't touch!
You'll get in dutch!

MAN (in astonishment, to audience) What did
that butterfly say?

AUDIENCE (singing) Hands off! Don't touch!
I don't ask much—Hands off! Don't touch!

You'll get in dutch!

**While the MAN is listening to the audience, the
BUTTERFLY tiptoes away. When the MAN looks
around, the BUTTERFLY is gone.**

MAN That butterfly wouldn't fit in my
net anyway!

Enter LION. Leaps onto stage, confronting the MAN.

MAN By George! It's a two-legged

LION

little box

big box

final shape

Get a box that is large
enough to cover the
whole body so just the
feet show. You will also
need a small box.
Outline eyes, nose, and
mouth on small box. For
lion mane use pieces of
twine. Dip it in watered-
down Elmer's glue and
glue all over front of box.
Small holes for seeing
and speaking can be
made where they serve
best. Lion's mane will
cover them.

BUTTERFLY

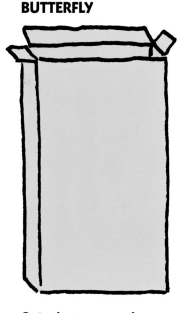

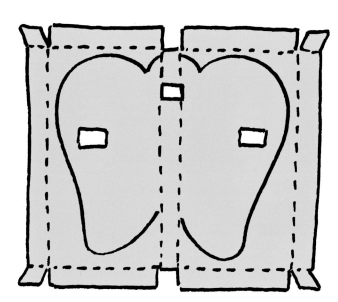

Get a large narrow box.

Split box and open.

Cut on dotted line.
Cut holes in each wing
to hold butterfly, and
cut a center hole to
look or talk through.
Folds in cardboard
allow wings to flap.
Because it is held by
hands, costume can
move up, down, and
sideways.

man-eating *Leo furioso*!

The MAN is frightened and backs away. The LION follows him slowly around the stage. It's very slow and scary. Suddenly the LION pounces and the MAN falls to his knees.

LION I AM GOING TO EAT YOU!!!

MAN Eat me if you must, but before you do, may I please say a few last words?

LION GRRR—SURE—RRRR.

MAN Hands off! Don't touch!
I don't ask much—Hands off! Don't touch!

You'll get in dutch!

LION (to audience) What did that man say?

AUDIENCE (shouting) Hands off! Don't touch!
I don't ask much—Hands off! Don't touch!
You'll get in dutch!

While the audience is shouting, the MAN tiptoes away offstage. When the song is over, the LION realizes the MAN has gone and runs offstage after him. The MAN runs back with the LION chasing him. They run around and around. The MAN escapes by running offstage. The LION is confused, roars, and runs off in the other direction.

I WON'T TAKE A BATH!

COSTUMES

BATHTUB. A large cardboard cutout shaped and painted to look like a bathtub. The bathtub should be about five feet long, but the size can be adjusted to accommodate a small actor.

SOAP. An oversize cardboard cutout the shape of a soap bar. It should be large enough to cover a kneeling actor with only head and shoulders showing.

PETER. An oversize painted cardboard cutout of a boy. It should be at least two feet taller than the actor who holds it. The cardboard folds at the hips and knees. The folds enable PETER to sit in the bathtub. Attached to the back is a large wooden handle. The actor behind the cutout can move the figure without ever being seen. The back of the cardboard is painted pink to look as if Peter were naked.

MOTHER. An oversize cardboard cutout, much taller than PETER and painted to look like a very large motherly woman. Probably two or more cardboard cartons opened and flattened can be put together with masking tape and braced with a wood lathe. On the back of the MOTHER are large wooden handles. Two people can get behind the MOTHER to move her. The voice of the MOTHER is best handled by an offstage microphone.

THE END. A flat, thin box such as a card table might come in. The bottom is cut out and THE END is painted on it. It is actually possible for an actor to get in it with only his legs showing. The effect is very humorous.

I WON'T TAKE A BATH!

Entrance Music

Moderate

Music by
DONALD ASHWANDER

(Bathtub enters)

(Soap enters)

(Bathtub: Spoken in rhythm)

I am a bath - tub.___ stal-wart and true,

(Soap: Spoken in rhythm)

Stand-ing here wait-ing on the bath room floor. ____ I am a soap bar,

firm and square, and I take my job very se - ri - ous - ly.

Waltz tempo

Tub & soap: Oh, please take a bath. Oh, please take a bath. Oh,
Peter: I won't take a bath. I won't take a bath. I

please take a bath to - day. _____ Oh,
won't take a bath to - day. _____ I

please take a bath. Oh, please take a bath. Oh,
won't take a bath. I won't take a bath. I

please take a bath. to - day.
won't take a bath. to - day.

GENERAL DESCRIPTION OF MOVEMENT

Because of the size of the cardboard cutouts and because the actors are either largely or completely covered by them, the cutouts should move slightly each time a character speaks. This makes it easier for the audience to know which character is speaking.

MUSIC
Enter BATHTUB, lumbering downstage right in time with the music. BATHTUB stops. Enter SOAP, scurrying to stage right and stopping in front of the BATHTUB.

BATHTUB I am a bathtub, stalwart and true, standing here waiting on the bathroom floor.

SOAP I am a soap bar, firm and square, and I take my job very seriously.

BATHTUB and SOAP And we're here to give Peter his bath.

SOAP Where is that boy?

BATHTUB He's in a bad mood.

SOAP He hates to take baths.

BATHTUB And he's terribly rude.

MUSIC
Enter PETER. He also stops downstage, but to the side of BATHTUB and SOAP.

PETER Were you speaking to me? I heard what you said. I won't take a bath! I'd rather be dead!

MUSIC
BATHTUB and SOAP (singing, while moving closer and closer to PETER)
Oh, please take a bath,
Oh, please take a bath,
Oh, please take a bath today.
Oh, please take a bath,
Oh, please take a bath,
Oh, please take a bath today.

MUSIC stops.

PETER No!

BATHTUB and SOAP Yes!

PETER No!

BATHTUB and SOAP Yes!!

PETER No!!

BATHTUB and SOAP (Return to their original place.) YEEEEEEES!

PETER (Comes downstage to the audience.) My voice is so little, and theirs are so loud! Besides, it's two against one. I need help! Everybody who hates to take baths, sing with me—"I won't take a bath today!"

MUSIC
PETER and AUDIENCE (singing, while PETER moves in time to music) I won't take a bath, I won't take a bath, I won't take a bath today. I won't take a bath, I won't take a bath, I won't take a bath today.

MUSIC stops.

SOAP What'll we do, Tub?

BATHTUB You talk to him, Soap, he'll listen to you.

SOAP tiptoes stage left to PETER.

SOAP Peter, Peter dear . . . don't you want to be clean?

PETER Never in my life!

SOAP scurries back to its original position.

SOAP I told you he wouldn't; he's terribly mean.

BATHTUB We need help!

SOAP and BATHTUB move downstage to audience.

BATHTUB Listen, everybody! You've heard what he said.

SOAP He won't take a bath, he'd rather be dead.

BATHTUB Now you've heard our song!

SOAP Sing along with us!

SOAP and BATHTUB Oh, please take a bath today.

MUSIC
SOAP, BATHTUB, and AUDIENCE sing. SOAP and BATHTUB rock back and forth.

Oh, please take a bath,
Oh, please take a bath,
Oh, please take a bath today.
Oh, please take a bath,
Oh, please take a bath,
Oh, please take a bath today.

PETER I will never take a bath! (Actor spins figure in the air and sets it down decisively. This is not as difficult as it sounds, because the figure is rigid.)

SOAP Wait until your mother comes, young man!

BATHTUB You'll change your tune.

PETER We'll see about that! (Actor kicks PETER's legs forward, and PETER sits down on the floor.)

MUSIC
Enter MOTHER from upstage. She moves center stage on music cue. The voice of MOTHER comes from an offstage microphone while the cardboard cutout shifts back and forth at center stage as if speaking.

MOTHER Peter, aren't you in your bath yet? Just what is taking you so long?

PETER I was just getting ready, Mother! (Actor lifts PETER up and turns cardboard around.)

PETER jumps into the bathtub. He now looks as if he is sitting in the tub (because of the fold at the knees), and the audience can see only his shoulders and head.

MOTHER Poor Peter, he just hates to take a bath. Well, I was exactly the same when I was a child. I even made up a song about it. Let's all sing it!

ALL (singing)
I won't take a bath,
I won't take a bath,
I won't take a bath today.
I won't take a bath,
I won't take a bath,
I won't take a bath today.

I won't take a bath,
I won't take a bath,
I won't take a bath today.
I won't take a bath,
I won't take a bath,
I won't take a bath today.

As "I Won't Take a Bath!" concludes, THE END enters, running around the stage. The actors onstage come out from behind their cardboard cutouts, lean them against MOTHER, and chase the cardboard box. They catch the box and lift it off the actor underneath. The cast members bow and exit with their cardboard cutouts, on music cue. The actor who was under the sign lifts it with THE END facing the audience and exits, holding up sign triumphantly.

CHARACTERS
TREE
FATHER
MOTHER
CHILD
BIG BURGER
ICE CREAM

Burger

PROPS

TREE. A cardboard cutout of a tree trunk with a leafy top. It should be large enough to hide an actor and light enough for an actor to hold.

CAR. Two pieces of cardboard, 6 feet long and 3 feet wide attached at both ends so that it can enclose three actors. If the actors are small, the car can be smaller. One side has a door that can open; it is kept closed with Velcro. The car is painted yellow with a black outline and black door and wheels.

LOLLIPOP (for **CHILD**). A cardboard circle, painted, and glued to a stick.

BIG BURGER and **ICE CREAM.** Cardboard signs about 3 x 2 1/2 feet. Again, for small actors the signs can be smaller. Each should cover the actor's head and shoulders and be light enough to be easily held. Both should be painted with garish colors and should look like advertisements.

WRAPPED BIG BURGER. A 45-foot length of 5-foot-wide white paper rolled up into a huge ball. At one end of the paper is a small pocket for the hamburger.

HAMBURGER. A 2-inch real cookie.

The tree, the ice cream, and the Big Burger are props that must be handled by an actor.

SETTING

TREE enters and moves up and down with a small, bouncy, rhythmic movement suggesting a moving landscape. When TREE reaches center stage it bounces in place. Enter FATHER, MOTHER, and CHILD (pretending to lick the lollipop), looking pleased to be going on a trip. They get into the car. Car also bounces slightly as if on a bumpy road. It stops near TREE.

MOTHER Well, here we are, ready at last to start our big trip across the country.

CHILD Ma and Pa, how far is it to the Grand Canyon?

FATHER It's a long way off, dear.

MOTHER But first we have to get to the highway. Step on the gas.

FATHER We're off!

Car with happy family moves across stage. TREE moves in opposite direction and exits. Car crosses back and forth across stage. MOTHER and CHILD look from side to side as if passing beautiful scenery. FATHER looks straight ahead as if driving. Suddenly BIG BURGER (an actor holding the sign) jumps onstage from the wing.

BIG BURGER (always speaks in a loud, commanding voice) Big Burger.

CHILD Ma and Pa, look! There's a talking sign.

BIG BURGER Get your Big Burger!

CHILD Can we have a Big Burger for lunch today?

MOTHER Angel, you just had breakfast.

CHILD I want a Big Burger!

FATHER I'll tell you what. We'll start our trip off with a little treat. Besides, I'm hungry myself.

CHILD Goody.

BIG BURGER disappears behind wing. Car moves downstage, then loops upstage. Suddenly BIG BURGER jumps onstage from a wing on opposite side of the stage.

BIG BURGER Big Burger!

CHILD There's the sign again! On top of a hill.

MOTHER I am not going up that hill.

FATHER Why did we buy this new car if we can't climb up a little hill?

CHILD Ma, the Grand Canyon has much bigger hills than that.

MOTHER All right, you can go up, but I'm not looking.

BIG BURGER disappears. Front of car lifts up. Family leans back as if going uphill. They are thrown forward, then backward, as car lurches and swerves.

MOTHER (shouts) Reverse! Go back!

FATHER It's stuck.

CHILD I'm falling out!

MOTHER Stop, stop!

FATHER Hold tight!

Car lunges forward and stops.

FATHER Now where did that Big Burger go?

MOTHER This whole thing is a wild-goose chase.

CHILD But I want a Big Burger!

MOTHER Do you want a Big Burger or do you want the Grand Canyon?

BIG BURGER Big Burger!

Car backs up, then changes direction, then swerves to side. Family shouts. BIG BURGER moves about stage, constantly eluding car.

CHILD Back up, Poppy!

MOTHER Don't back up on the highway.

FATHER I see it, I see it.

Car spins in a circle. Car loops around stage and stops near BIG BURGER. Family, exhausted, leans against one another.

BIG BURGER You are here.

Family straightens and brightens.

FAMILY We're here.

FATHER (Opens car door. **To MOTHER**) Come out, darling. (**to CHILD**) Get out, angel.

CHILD Oh, Poppy, I'm so excited!

Family moves even closer to sign.

BIG BURGER Your hamburger dream has come true!

The ball of white paper is lifted slowly over the top of the sign. The family raises their arms to get it. They gently place it on the ground.

MOTHER It's bigger than I thought.

FATHER It sure is.

CHILD I want it, I want it!

The family unwraps the Big Burger with joyful dance-like movements, tossing paper in the air. As paper covers the stage, CHILD dances with it. As FATHER unrolls the last few yards of paper, the action slows. At the very end of the length of paper, FATHER finds the cookie tucked into the pocket.

FATHER (holding up cookie) Here it is.

MOTHER Is this our hamburger dream come true?

FATHER Some surprise. **(Gives cookie to MOTHER.)**

MOTHER (to CHILD) Here, dear, you can have it.

CHILD takes it, looks at it for a moment, then wails.

FATHER (to MOTHER) Come on, dear, let's go. Let's get out of here.

MOTHER What are we going to do with this paper? We can't just leave it on the highway.

FATHER We'll pick it up and take it with us.

MOTHER (helping FATHER gather paper) Oh, all right.

FATHER (to CHILD) Get in the car, angel.

CHILD (getting into car) I never get anything I want.

MOTHER and FATHER, with all the paper in their arms, stuff it into car, inadvertently covering CHILD. Then they get into car and close door.

CHILD (from under paper) I can't breathe!

MOTHER (not noticing paper over CHILD's face) That's all right, dear.

CHILD pulls paper away from her face. Looks glum.

MOTHER Now let's cheer up. Let's start this whole trip again.

CHILD How far is it now to the Grand Canyon?

FATHER It's still a long way off.

MOTHER But first we have to get back to the highway.

ICE CREAM (Jumps onto stage, holding painted sign, and speaks with the same commanding voice as BIG BURGER's.) Ice-cream cone.

CHILD Ice cream!

MOTHER That looks good!

FATHER Let's get it!

ICE CREAM loops around stage and exits. Family in car, with paper trailing, rushes after it.

CHILD Ice cream! I love ice cream!
Family in car exits.

Create a poster for your show. Here are examples of those you might make for the plays in this book, but you can design them any way you like, with the names of the real actors. Your poster can placed on a bulletin board in your school, outside a theater, or in your living room—depending on where you perform your play.

On the far right are examples of some styles of lettering you may follow.

If your poster will sit on the floor it should be drawn or pasted on cardboard with a piece of cardboard taped on the back to form an easel (*right*).

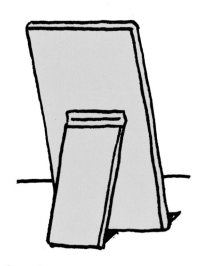

back of poster

Costume and Prop Ideas

Cardboard boxes can make a lot of different things.

Cat This costume can be made by using a cardboard box with a person bent over inside.

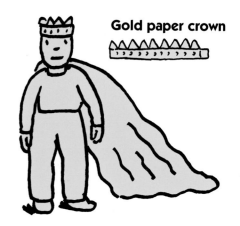

Gold paper crown

Kingly robe Wear an old drape or dark bedsheet.

Turtle A box with a person kneeling inside.

Fairy Attach waxed paper streamers to cardboard wings. The wand might be a yardstick with a gold paper star.

Old Man
Paint a long piece of brown paper white. Get an old hat from a closet and a stick. Put on the hat, attach the beard, and use the stick for a cane.

Princess An old lace tablecloth with a hole in the middle for head and holes for arms works well.

If you want to look as if you're in **bed**, stand behind printed fabric.

A **broom** can be a hand-held mask.

So can a **frying pan**.

A house can be built using an empty refrigerator box.

An upside-down **pocketbook** makes a funny hat.

Flexible plastic pipe worn on arms and legs makes a **man from outer space.**

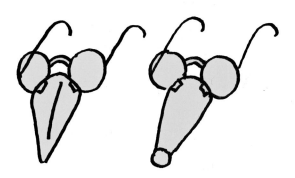

A pair of **eyeglasses** with attached beak makes a **chicken** or a **fox.**

CREDITS

Front cover
(left to right) Alan Johnson,
Ted Brackett, Jade Jenkins,
Tyrone Grant, Brenda Cummings
Photos by Jonathan Atkins

Page 6
Jade Jenkins (left),
Tyrone Grant
Photo by Gerry Goodstein

Page 7 (top)
Judith Martin
Photo by Lynn Saville

Page 7 (bottom)
Joyce Lee
Photo by Gerry Goodstein

Page 8
Irving Burton
Photo by Paul Berg

Page 9 (top)
Judith Martin (left),
Jeanne Michels
Photo by Ken Howard

Page 9 (bottom)
Brenda Cummings (left),
Judith Martin
Photo by Martha Swope

Page 10 (top)
Jan Maxwell (left),
Brenda Cummings
Photo by Ken Howard

Page 10 (center)
(left to right) Judith Martin,
Daniel Wilkes Kelley,
Ted Brackett, Jeanne Michels
Photo by Martha Swope

Page 10 (bottom)
Tyrone Grant (left), Ted Brackett
Photo by Gerry Goodstein

Page 11
Judith Martin
Photo by Martha Swope

Page 12
(left to right) Judith Martin,
Peter Guttmacher, Jan Maxwell
Photo by Ken Howard

Page 13 (top)
(left to right) Irving Burton,
Jeanne Michels, Cort Miller
Photo by Ken Howard

Page 13 (bottom)
(left to right) Brenda Cummings,
Judith Martin,
Irving Burton (behind box)
Photo by Ken Howard

Page 33
Photos by Jonathan Atkins

Back cover
Ted Brackett
Photo by Jonathan Atkins